RANJOT SINGH CHAHAL

Why I Always Ask

Curious Minds, Bright Futures, and Lifelong Learning

Rana Books

First published by Rana Books (UK, INDIA) 2023

First edition

ISBN: 978-81-19786-19-0

Contents

Chapter 1: The Curiosity-driven Mind

The curiosity-driven mind is an insatiable seeker of knowledge, perpetually driven by the thrill of discovery. It finds wonder in the intricate details of the everyday and the profound mysteries of the cosmos, constantly pushing boundaries to understand the world and its complexities. This ever-curious mind is an endless source of inspiration, sparking innovation and creativity in its unending quest to unravel the secrets of existence.

1.1 The Nature of Curiosity

Curiosity is the innate drive to seek knowledge explore the unknown and understand the world around us. It is an essential aspect of human nature that emerges early in childhood and continues throughout our lives. Curiosity can be seen as a combination of perceptual curiosity which is the desire to explore new sensory experiences and epistemic curiosity which is the desire to acquire knowledge and understand complex concepts.

1.2 Why Do I Always Ask Questions?

Asking questions is a fundamental part of human cognition and learning. It allows us to explore new ideas challenge assumptions and deepen our understanding of the world. Questioning is a cognitive process that enables us to fill gaps in our knowledge and make connections between different pieces of information.

When we ask questions we engage in critical thinking and problem-solving. We analyze situations evaluate evidence and seek new perspectives. Asking questions also promotes creativity and innovation as it encourages us to think beyond conventional wisdom and explore alternative possibilities.

1.3 The Benefits of Being Inquisitive

The benefits of cultivating a curiosity-driven mindset are numerous and far-reaching:

1.3.1 Intellectual Growth:

Curiosity fuels intellectual growth by motivating us to seek knowledge and understanding. As we ask questions and actively engage with new ideas we expand our intellectual horizons and develop a broader perspective. Curiosity-driven learning enhances our cognitive abilities enhances memory retention and improves our problem-solving skills.

For example a student who is curious about history may engage in extensive research read various sources and critically analyze different perspectives. This process not only deepens their understanding of historical events but also hones their research and analytical skills.

1.3.2 Personal Development:

Curiosity is closely linked to personal development as it encourages self-reflection and introspection. By asking questions about ourselves and our beliefs we gain a deeper understanding of our values strengths and weaknesses. This self-awareness can lead to personal growth improved decision-making and increased self-confidence.

For instance someone who is curious about their emotional responses may explore the field of psychology attend therapy sessions or engage in introspective practices like journaling. Through these activities they can gain insights into their emotions develop healthy coping mechanisms and improve their overall well-being.

1.3.3 Adaptability and Resilience:

Being curious allows us to adapt and thrive in an ever-changing world. Curiosity drives us to explore new environments learn new skills and adapt to unfamiliar circumstances. It fosters a growth mindset which is the belief that abilities and intelligence can be developed through effort and learning.

Consider an employee who is curious about emerging technologies in their industry. They actively seek out opportunities to learn and adapt attending workshops participating in online courses and experimenting with new tools. Their curiosity-driven approach enables them to stay ahead of the curve and navigate changes in their field more effectively.

1.3.4 Innovation and Creativity:

Curiosity is the wellspring of innovation and creativity. By questioning the status quo and exploring uncharted territories we can uncover new insights and generate novel ideas. Curiosity-driven individuals are more likely to think outside the box challenge existing paradigms and develop innovative solutions to complex problems.

Take the example of a scientist who is curious about unlocking the secrets of the universe. Their insatiable curiosity motivates them to conduct experiments explore new theories and push the boundaries of knowledge. Through their inquisitive mind-set they make groundbreaking discoveries and contribute to scientific advancements.

1.4 Cultivating a Curiosity-driven Mindset

Cultivating a curiosity-driven mindset involves embracing curiosity as an inherent part of our lives and actively nurturing it. Here are some strategies to develop and sustain a curiosity-driven mindset:

1.4.1 Embrace the Unknown:

Curiosity thrives in the realm of uncertainty. Embrace the unknown and see it as an opportunity for growth and discovery. Instead of fearing failure or making assumptions approach new experiences with an open mind and a willingness to explore.

For instance rather than avoiding a challenging project at work due to fear of failure embrace the opportunity to learn and grow. Ask questions seek guidance and approach it with curiosity knowing that mistakes and setbacks are an inherent part of the learning process.

1.4.2 Ask Thought-provoking Questions:

Develop the habit of asking thought-provoking questions in your daily life. Challenge assumptions seek deeper understanding and explore different perspectives. This can be applied to various aspects of life from personal relationships to professional endeavors.

For example if you are engaged in a debate about a social issue ask questions that encourage critical thinking and promote a deeper understanding of the topic. By delving into the underlying factors and complexities you can gain insights and broaden your perspective.

1.4.3 Pursue New Experiences:

Engage in activities that expose you to new knowledge and experiences. Travel to different places read diverse books attend seminars and workshops or engage in hobbies outside your comfort zone. By exposing yourself to diverse perspectives and novel situations you stimulate your curiosity and expand your horizons.

For instance if you have always been interested in painting but never pursued it enroll in a painting class or experiment with different mediums. By embracing a new experience you ignite your curiosity and tap into your creative potential.

1.4.4 Foster a Learning Culture:

Create an environment that encourages curiosity and lifelong learning. Surround yourself with curious individuals who value knowledge and intellectual growth. Engage in discussions debates and collaborative projects that stimulate curiosity and foster a love for learning.

For example you can join a book club attend workshops or participate in online forums related to your interests. By actively engaging with a community of curious individuals you can exchange ideas gain insights and fuel your own curiosity.

Conclusion

Curiosity is a fundamental aspect of being human. It drives our intellectual growth personal development adaptability and creativity. By cultivating a curiosity-driven mindset we can unlock our full potential and lead fulfilling and meaningful lives. Embrace the unknown ask thought-provoking questions pursue new experiences and foster a learning culture to continuously nourish your curiosity and expand your horizons. In doing so you embark on a lifelong journey of exploration discovery and intellectual growth.

Chapter 2: The Quest for Knowledge

The quest for knowledge is an unwavering journey of the mind, an unrelenting pursuit of understanding that spans the breadth of human curiosity. It drives individuals to explore the known and venture into the unknown, seeking answers to the questions that define our existence. This relentless pursuit not only enriches our understanding of the world but also fuels innovation and progress, inspiring generations to reach for new heights in the pursuit of wisdom and insight.

2.1 The Motivation to Learn

Learning is an inherent human instinct. From a young age we are naturally curious and driven to understand the world around us. This curiosity is fueled by our innate desire for knowledge and the need to make sense of our surroundings. The motivation to learn is not only driven by the acquisition of information but also by the desire to improve ourselves solve problems and make a positive impact on the world.

The motivation to learn can stem from various sources. It could be sparked by personal interests such as a fascination with space exploration a passion for art or a love for languages. It can also be driven by challenges we encounter in our daily lives like understanding complex concepts at work navigating personal relationships or overcoming obstacles.

For example consider a person who wants to learn how to play a musical instrument. Their motivation could arise from a deep love for music a desire for self-expression or even the aspiration to become a professional musician. Similarly a student studying math might be motivated by the thrill of solving complex problems or the need to excel in their academic pursuits.

2.2 Seeking Answers and Solutions

In our quest for knowledge we are constantly seeking answers and solutions to questions and problems. This process involves actively engaging with the subject matter exploring different sources of information and critically analyzing the available knowledge. Whether it is through reading books conducting experiments or engaging in discussions seeking answers requires a proactive approach.

Seeking answers and solutions enables us to understand the world better make informed decisions and address challenges effectively. The desire to find answers can arise from a range of circumstances including a personal dilemma the need for clarity in a confusing situation or scientific curiosity.

For example imagine a person who is trying to understand the impact of climate change on coastal ecosystems. They might embark on a journey of research seeking answers by studying scholarly articles attending conferences and even conducting fieldwork. Their dedication and exploration will allow them to acquire the necessary insights to comprehend the complex dynamics at play propose solutions and contribute to the broader understanding of the subject.

2.3 The Power of Questioning

One of the most fundamental tools we have for seeking answers is questioning. Questioning allows us to challenge assumptions probe deeper into matters and uncover hidden truths. It is through asking questions that we stimulate critical thinking expand our understanding and make new discoveries.

Questioning can take various forms ranging from simple inquiries to more complex and thought-provoking queries. It involves both questioning existing knowledge and posing hypothetical questions to explore new possibilities. The power of questioning lies in its ability to challenge the status quo push boundaries and pave the way for innovation and progress.

For example in the field of physics the question "What is the nature of light?" led scientists to explore and discover its dual nature as both particles and waves. This concept known as wave-particle duality revolutionized our understanding of the nature of light and laid the foundation for quantum mechanics.

Furthermore questioning can also play a crucial role in personal and professional development. By questioning our assumptions beliefs and behaviors we can foster personal growth deepen our self-awareness and challenge the limitations we place upon ourselves.

2.4 When Asking Leads to Discoveries

Throughout history many groundbreaking discoveries and inventions have emerged through the act of asking questions. Innovators scientists and thinkers from various fields have unleashed the power of curiosity and questioning to redefine our understanding of the world.

For instance the question "Why do objects fall to the ground?" posed by Isaac Newton led to his formulation of the laws of motion and the law of universal gravitation. This groundbreaking work revolutionized the field of physics and laid the foundation for modern-day classical mechanics.

Similarly the question "Can we travel to the moon?" sparked the Apollo space program and eventually led to the first manned moon landing in 1969. The pursuit of this question opened up new possibilities in human exploration and reshaped our understanding of space travel.

But not all discoveries are confined to scientific or technological realms. Questioning can also lead to profound insights in philosophical social and artistic domains. For example Friedrich Nietzsche's question "What is the meaning of life?" challenged traditional religious and moral values leading to a profound shift in philosophical thought during the late 19th century.

In conclusion the quest for knowledge is a fundamental aspect of the human experience. It is driven by our innate curiosity the desire to improve ourselves and the need to find answers and solutions. Through questioning we can challenge assumptions deepen our understanding and make groundbreaking discoveries. The act of seeking answers and solutions not only expands our intellectual horizons but also empowers us to navigate life's complexities and make a positive impact on the world. So let us embrace the power of questioning and embark on a lifelong journey of learning and discovery.

Chapter 3: Expand Your Understanding

Expanding your understanding is a transformative journey of personal growth and enlightenment. It involves a deliberate and continuous effort to broaden your knowledge, perspectives, and horizons. Embracing this path empowers you to see the world through different lenses, fostering empathy, tolerance, and open-mindedness. By engaging in diverse experiences, learning from various sources, and embracing lifelong learning, you embark on a profound adventure that enriches your life and equips you to navigate the complexities of an ever-evolving world with wisdom and insight.

3.1 Embracing Different Perspectives:

To expand our understanding it is essential to embrace different perspectives. This involves actively seeking out diverse view-points and considering alternative ways of thinking. By doing so we can broaden our horizons and gain a more comprehensive understanding of various topics.

One example of embracing different perspectives is through cul-tural immersion. By immersing ourselves in different cultures we can gain insights into unique worldviews belief systems and values. For instance traveling to a foreign country and engaging with the local people can expose us to new customs traditions and ways of life. This firsthand experience can challenge our own preconceived notions and help us develop a more nuanced understanding of different cultures.

Another example is seeking out diverse sources of information. In today's interconnected world we have access to a vast amount of information from various mediums such as books articles podcasts and social media. However it is important to be critical consumers of information and actively seek out multiple perspectives on a given topic. By doing so we can avoid confirmation bias and gain a more balanced understanding of complex issues.

Furthermore engaging in respectful dialogue with individuals who hold different opinions can also broaden our understanding. Through open and respectful conversations we can exchange ideas challenge our own assumptions and gain new insights. This can be done through participating in debates attending conferences or joining online forums centered around specific topics. By actively listening and considering alternative viewpoints we can enhance our understanding and foster intellectual growth.

3.2 Challenging Assumptions and Beliefs:

Challenging assumptions and beliefs is a crucial aspect of expanding our understanding. It involves examining our existing beliefs critically and being open to the possibility of different perspectives. By questioning assumptions we can prevent stagnation in our understanding and encourage intellectual growth.

One example of challenging assumptions is in the field of science. Scientific progress often occurs when researchers question established theories and assumptions. For instance when the theory of continental drift was proposed by Alfred Wegener in the early 20th century it challenged the prevailing belief of a static Earth. Despite facing initial skepticism Wegener's theory eventually led to the development of our understanding of plate tectonics revolutionizing the field of geology.

In a personal context challenging assumptions can involve questioning our own deeply held beliefs and biases. We all have individual perspectives shaped by our upbringing societal influences and personal experiences. By critically evaluating these beliefs we can identify any inherent biases or limitations that may hinder our understanding. This self-reflection can help us overcome cognitive biases and develop a more objective and open-minded approach to learning.

Additionally challenging assumptions can be applied in analyzing societal issues. Often we hold certain assumptions about social economic or political systems without critically evaluating their effectiveness. By challenging these assumptions we can gain a more comprehensive understanding of these systems' strengths and weaknesses. This critical analysis can lead to innovative solutions and societal progress.

3.3 Embodying a Growth Mindset:

To expand our understanding it is crucial to embody a growth mindset. A growth mindset is the belief that our abilities and intelligence can be developed through effort practice and learning. By adopting a growth mindset we can overcome challenges persist in the face of setbacks and continuously improve our understanding.

One example of embodying a growth mindset is in the context of learning new skills. When we approach learning with a growth mindset we view challenges as opportunities for growth rather than obstacles. For instance suppose we are learning to play a musical instrument. Instead of giving up when faced with difficult pieces of music a growth mindset encourages us to persist practice regularly and seek guidance from experienced musicians. Through continued effort and a belief in our ability to improve we can expand our musical understanding and proficiency.

In a professional context a growth mindset can also drive innovation and success. Embracing challenges and seeking opportunities for continuous learning can lead to creative problem-solving and adaptability. For example individuals with a growth mindset are more likely to seek feedback learn from their mistakes and actively pursue development opportunities. This mindset enables them to continuously evolve their understanding and skills leading to professional growth and advancement.

Furthermore a growth mindset can positively impact interpersonal relationships. When we approach interactions with others from a growth mindset perspective we value constructive feedback embrace different perspectives and are willing to engage in collaborative problem-solving. This mindset fosters a culture of learning and mutual growth enabling deeper connections and understanding between individuals.

3.4 Continuously Evolving through Inquiry:

To expand our understanding we must adopt a mindset of continuous inquiry. This involves asking questions seeking answers and actively engaging in the process of learning. By continually seeking new knowledge and perspectives we can adapt and evolve our understanding over time.

Inquiry-based learning is an effective method for expanding our understanding. It involves actively investigating a topic asking questions and conducting research to find answers. For example a student studying history may formulate research questions analyze primary sources and critically evaluate different historical interpretations. Through this process they can develop a deeper and more nuanced understanding of historical events and their significance.

Inquiry can also be applied in problem-solving. Instead of passively accepting a problem at face value individuals with an inquiry mindset ask probing questions to gain a comprehensive understanding of the problem's underlying causes and potential solutions. This approach allows for creative and innovative problem-solving by considering multiple perspectives and exploring different strategies.

Additionally inquiry can be applied in real-world contexts such as within scientific research. Scientists constantly question existing theories conduct experiments and analyze data to expand our understanding of the natural world. The scientific method built on curiosity and inquiry has led to significant advancements in various fields from medicine to technology.

Moreover inquiry-based approaches can be applied in everyday life. By cultivating a sense of curiosity and being open to new ideas we can continuously expand our understanding. This can involve exploring new hobbies reading diverse literature engaging in artistic endeavors or seeking out new experiences. Through active inquiry we can deepen our understanding of ourselves others and the world around us.

In conclusion expanding our understanding requires embracing different perspectives challenging assumptions and beliefs embodying a growth mindset and continuously evolving through inquiry. By actively seeking out diverse viewpoints critically evaluating our beliefs believing in our capacity for growth and engaging in continuous inquiry we can develop a more comprehensive and nuanced understanding of various topics. This not only enhances our personal growth but also contributes to a more informed and interconnected society.

Chapter 4: Finding Your Passion

Finding your passion is a deeply introspective quest that leads you to uncover the core pursuits that ignite your soul with purpose and enthusiasm. It entails exploring your interests, strengths, and values, often through trial and error, until you discover the activities and causes that resonate with your innermost self. This journey of self-discovery not only brings joy and fulfillment but also fuels dedication and commitment to pursuing your chosen path with unwavering zeal. As you align your life with your passion, you unlock the potential for a meaningful and purpose-driven existence, where each day becomes an opportunity to live out your true calling.

4.1 Exploring Boundaries and Interests

Finding your passion is an essential step in self-discovery and personal fulfillment. Many individuals spend a significant portion of their lives searching for their true passions often feeling unfulfilled or lacking direction until they discover what truly ignites their spirit. In this chapter we will delve into various strategies and techniques that can help you identify and cultivate your passions.

One effective way to begin your passion exploration journey is by exploring the boundaries of your comfort zone and expanding your horizons. Often individuals are not aware of their true passions and interests because they haven't ventured beyond their familiar surroundings. Stepping outside of your comfort zone allows you to experience new things meet different people and gain fresh perspectives all of which can ignite passion within you.

For example let's say you have always been interested in art but have never actively pursued it. By taking an art class or visiting art galleries you can expose yourself to various art forms and styles. This exposure may spark a deep passion for a particular form of art such as painting or sculpting that you were previously unaware of.

Additionally it is crucial to pay attention to the activities or topics that naturally captivate your attention and curiosity. Often when you are genuinely interested in something you tend to devote more time and energy to it without feeling exhausted or bored. These areas of interest can serve as clues to your underlying passions.

For instance if you find yourself spending hours researching and reading about sustainable living it might indicate a strong passion for environmental conservation. By exploring this further you could discover opportunities to engage in activities related to sustainability such as joining local environmental organizations or participating in community clean-up efforts.

4.2 Uncovering Hidden Passions and Talents

Sometimes your true passions and talents are hidden beneath layers of societal expectations or personal insecurities. Society often emphasizes practicality and conformity which can discourage you from pursuing unconventional or less financially lucrative passions. However discovering your authentic passions requires breaking free from these constraints and allowing yourself to explore the things that genuinely excite and inspire you.

Consider revisiting your childhood and the activities that brought you joy and fulfillment. Often when we were younger our passions were not influenced by societal expectations or financial considerations. Reflecting on these experiences can help unearth hidden passions that have been overshadowed by adulthood responsibilities.

For example perhaps you used to spend hours playing a musical instrument as a child but stopped because it was considered impractical as you got older. Revisiting this passion and exploring the possibility of reconnecting with music could reignite a deep-seated love for playing an instrument.

Furthermore paying attention to the activities that effortlessly absorb your attention and make you lose track of time can reveal hidden talents. These talents often come naturally to you and can signify areas where you excel and find joy.

For instance if you find pleasure in organizing and arranging things meticulously you might have a talent for interior design or event planning. Recognizing and acknowledging these talents can play a vital role in finding your passion and pursuing a fulfilling career or hobby.

4.3 The Role of Inquiry in Passion Discovery

Inquiry is a powerful tool for discovering your passions. Asking yourself thought-provoking questions can help uncover your core values interests and desires leading to a deeper understanding of what truly drives and inspires you.

Consider setting aside dedicated time for self-reflection and introspection. Use this time to ask yourself questions like:

- What activities make me lose track of time and feel fully engaged?
- What values and principles do I hold dear?
- What societal issues or causes resonate with me the most?
- What are the recurring themes in my dreams and aspirations?
- If I had unlimited resources and no constraints what would I pursue?

Taking the time to answer these questions honestly and critically can shed light on your underlying passions and guide you towards a more fulfilling life.

Additionally seeking external perspectives and feedback can provide valuable insights into your passions. Engaging in conversation and active listening with trusted friends family or mentors can help you gain new perspectives and identify patterns that you may have missed on your own.

4.4 Nurturing and Pursuing Your Passion

Once you have identified your passions it is crucial to nurture and actively pursue them. Passionate individuals often experience greater fulfillment a sense of purpose and increased motivation when they engage in activities aligned with their true passions.

One way to nurture your passion is by seeking opportunities for growth and learning within your chosen field. Engage in continuous education attend workshops conferences or join professional associations related to your passion. These activities not only enhance your skills but also connect you with like-minded individuals who share your passion.

For example if your passion lies in entrepreneurship you could attend business conferences enroll in entrepreneurship courses or join local networking groups. These activities expose you to new ideas provide learning opportunities and connect you with potential partners or mentors who can support your entrepreneurial journey.

Moreover integrating your passion into your daily life can spark inspiration and create a sense of purpose. Find ways to incorporate your passion into your work hobbies or side projects. This integration ensures that you are consistently engaged in activities aligned with your passions even if they are not your primary focus.

For instance if you are passionate about photography but currently work in a different field consider incorporating photography into your daily life by taking up photography projects during your free time or volunteering your skills for local events. This allows you to nurture your passion while maintaining stability in your current career.

Taking risks and embracing challenges are crucial elements of passion pursuit. Overcoming obstacles and pursuing opportunities outside of your comfort zone can accelerate your personal and professional growth and lead to greater levels of passion and fulfillment.

For instance if your passion lies in writing challenge yourself to submit your work to publications or start a blog to share your writing with a broader audience. Embracing these challenges pushes you to improve your skills build confidence and expand your reach.

In conclusion finding your passion requires exploration self-reflection and embracing new experiences. By expanding your horizons uncovering hidden talents practicing inquiry and nurturing your passions you can discover a deeper sense of fulfillment and purpose in life. It is through pursuing our passions that we unlock our true potential and make a meaningful impact on the world around us.

Chapter 5: The Art of Problem-Solving

The art of problem-solving is a dynamic and essential skill that empowers individuals to navigate life's challenges with creativity and efficacy. It involves identifying issues, breaking them down into manageable components, and devising innovative solutions. This art form combines analytical thinking, ingenuity, and adaptability, allowing one to approach problems from various angles and adapt strategies as needed. As you hone this skill, you become a masterful problem solver, capable of not only overcoming obstacles but also seizing opportunities, fostering resilience, and contributing to positive change in both your personal and professional spheres.

5.1 Identifying Problems and Obstacles

Problem-solving is an essential skill that we use in various aspects of our personal and professional lives. However before we can begin solving a problem we need to clearly identify what the problem is and understand the obstacles that may be preventing us from finding a solution.

Identifying problems requires a deep understanding of the situation at hand and the ability to recognize when something is not working as intended. This can involve analyzing data conducting research observing patterns and listening to feedback. It's important to approach problem identification with an open mind and a willingness to explore different perspectives and possibilities.

For example let's say you are a project manager tasked with improving the efficiency of a manufacturing process. You observe that there is a significant delay in the production line resulting in missed deadlines and increased costs. By analyzing the data and talking to the employees involved you identify that the problem is caused by a bottleneck in one particular machine. This bottleneck is preventing the smooth flow of materials and causing delays in the entire process.

In addition to identifying the problem it is crucial to recognize the obstacles that may impede the problem-solving process. Obstacles can take various forms such as limited resources conflicting priorities lack of information or resistance to change. Understanding these obstacles will allow you to develop strategies to overcome them and move forward with finding a solution.

Continuing with the example of the manufacturing process you might encounter obstacles such as budget constraints that prevent purchasing a new machine resistance from employees who are used to the current process or a lack of technical expertise to address the bottleneck effectively. Recognizing these obstacles helps you devise a plan to address each one and increases your chances of success.

5.2 Breaking Down Complex Issues

Complex problems can be overwhelming and difficult to tackle all at once. To effectively solve complex problems it is essential to break them down into smaller more manageable components. This process allows you to identify the root causes of the problem and develop a systematic approach to finding solutions.

Breaking down a problem involves analyzing its various aspects determining the relationships between these aspects and identifying the underlying causes and effects. This process helps to simplify the problem and allows you to focus your efforts on the most critical areas.

For example suppose you are a marketing manager tasked with boosting the sales of a specific product. The problem seems complex and multifaceted with several factors potentially affecting sales. By breaking down the problem you can identify factors such as pricing product positioning target audience and competition. You can then analyze each of these factors individually and determine the specific issues within each area.

Once you have broken down the problem into its components you can prioritize and address each component separately. By focusing on one aspect at a time you can delve deeper into the specific challenges and develop targeted solutions. This approach helps prevent overwhelm and allows for a more systematic problem-solving process.

5.3 Generating Creative Solutions

Effective problem-solving often requires thinking outside the box and generating creative solutions. Creativity involves producing new and innovative ideas that may not have been considered before. By expanding your thinking and considering alternative approaches you can discover fresh perspectives and find more effective solutions.

One way to foster creativity is to engage in brainstorming sessions with a diverse group of individuals. This approach encourages participants to freely contribute ideas without judgment or criticism. Brainstorming sessions allow for the exploration of multiple possibilities and the combination of different perspectives leading to more creative solutions.

For example imagine you are part of a team responsible for reducing customer complaints about a product. By holding a brainstorming session team members can share their ideas on how to address the issue. One person might suggest improving the product's quality while another may propose enhancing customer support. Someone else might suggest implementing a customer feedback system to identify trends and address concerns proactively. By drawing on a variety of ideas you can generate a range of potential solutions that may not have been considered individually.

Another way to foster creativity is through the use of techniques such as mind mapping or forced connections. Mind mapping involves visually mapping out ideas and concepts allowing for the exploration of various connections and associations. Forced connections involve linking seemingly unrelated ideas or concepts to find new and innovative solutions.

For instance let's say you are a software developer facing

a challenge in creating a user-friendly interface for a new application. By using mind mapping techniques you can visually map out the different elements of the interface and explore potential connections and relationships. Forced connections could involve drawing parallels between interface design principles and elements from unrelated fields such as architecture or graphic design to discover unique and innovative design solutions.

5.4 Applying Critical Thinking and Analysis

Critical thinking and analysis play a crucial role in problem-solving. These skills allow you to evaluate information identify assumptions consider alternative perspectives and make informed decisions.

Critical thinking involves actively questioning and challenging assumptions biases and preconceived ideas. It requires an open and objective mindset a willingness to consider different viewpoints and the ability to evaluate information based on its reliability and relevance.

Analytical thinking focuses on breaking down complex information identifying patterns and drawing logical conclusions. It allows you to synthesize data assess cause-and-effect relationships and identify trends or outliers.

When solving a problem critical thinking helps you examine the problem from different angles challenge assumptions and identify any potential biases that may be clouding your judgment. By questioning assumptions and considering alternative perspectives you can gain a deeper understanding of the problem and develop more effective solutions.

Analytical thinking on the other hand helps you make sense of the information available and identify the underlying causes of the problem. This allows you to develop targeted strategies that address the root causes rather than just treating the symptoms.

For example let's say you are a business owner trying to determine why sales have declined over the past few months. By applying critical thinking you might challenge the assumption that external factors such as market conditions are solely responsible for the decline. Instead you might consider factors such as changes in customer preferences or ineffective marketing strategies. Applying analytical thinking you can analyze sales data to identify trends customer feedback to uncover areas for improvement and market research to assess the competitive landscape. This data-driven and analytical approach allows you to develop strategies based on a deep understanding of the problem.

In conclusion the art of problem-solving involves several interconnected elements. It starts with identifying problems and obstacles breaking down complex issues into manageable components generating creative solutions and applying critical thinking and analysis to evaluate and implement those solutions. By honing these skills and leveraging various problem-solving strategies you can become a more effective problem solver in both personal and professional settings.

Chapter 6: Empowering Communication

Empowering communication is a potent tool that enables individuals to connect, inspire, and effect positive change in themselves and others. It involves fostering open and empathetic dialogues, actively listening, and articulating thoughts with clarity and conviction. Through this art, people can convey their ideas, emotions, and aspirations effectively, building bridges of understanding and trust. Empowering communication not only bolsters self-confidence but also uplifts those around us, encouraging collaboration and the realization of shared goals. In mastering this skill, individuals become catalysts for change, as their words and actions ignite motivation, promote inclusivity, and foster a culture of empowerment and growth.

6.1 Asking for Clarification and Understanding

In any conversation it is essential to ensure that both parties understand each other clearly. Asking for clarification and understanding helps clarify any confusion or misunderstandings that may arise during communication. This communication skill is particularly important when discussing complex or unfamiliar topics.

One way to ask for clarification is by seeking further information or explanation. For example if someone mentions a concept that you are unfamiliar with you can ask "Could you please explain that in more detail?" This prompts the speaker to provide additional information to aid your understanding.

Another way to seek clarification is by asking specific questions. For instance if the speaker uses a technical term that you are uncertain about you can ask "What do you mean by [term]?" This allows the speaker to provide a clear and concise definition of the unfamiliar term.

Asking for clarification not only promotes a better understanding of the topic being discussed but also demonstrates active engagement in the conversation. It shows that you are genuinely interested in understanding the speaker's message and encourages open and clear communication.

6.2 Active Listening and Engagement

Active listening is a crucial component of empowering communication. It involves fully concentrating on the speaker's words observing their non-verbal cues and being present in the moment. Active listening demonstrates respect for the speaker and their ideas creating a supportive and inclusive communication environment.

To practice active listening it is vital to eliminate distractions and focus solely on the speaker. This means putting away electronic devices making eye contact and maintaining an open posture. Additionally providing verbal and non-verbal feedback such as nodding or summarizing the speaker's main points shows that you are actively engaged and attentive.

Furthermore active listening involves being empathetic and understanding the speaker's perspective. Empathy allows you to connect with the speaker on an emotional level and demonstrate genuine care and concern. By actively listening and engaging in the conversation you create a safe space for open and effective communication.

6.3 Effective Questioning in Conversations

Effective questioning is a powerful communication tool that can facilitate deeper understanding and encourage critical thinking. By asking the right questions you can encourage the speaker to think more deeply about their message and provide further insights.

Open-ended questions are particularly effective in promoting meaningful conversations. Unlike closed-ended questions which can be answered with a simple "yes" or "no open-ended questions require the speaker to provide more detailed responses. For example instead of asking "Did you enjoy the presentation you can ask "What did you find most valuable about the presentation?" This type of question encourages the speaker to reflect on their experience and provide a more nuanced response.

Moreover reflective questions can be used to encourage the speaker to elaborate on their thoughts or feelings. By paraphrasing the speaker's statements and asking for confirmation or clarification you demonstrate active listening and promote a deeper understanding of their message. For instance if the speaker says "I was really frustrated with the lack of communication from the team you could respond with "So you felt frustrated because you didn't receive updates from the team regularly?"

However it is essential to ask questions with genuine curiosity and without judgment. Stereotyping or asking leading questions can hinder open and honest communication. Instead focus on asking neutral and thought-provoking questions that encourage dialogue and exploration.

6.4 Building Meaningful Connections through Inquiry

Inquiry-based communication involves actively seeking to understand others' perspectives and experiences. Instead of making assumptions or jumping to conclusions inquiry-based communication fosters curiosity and a willingness to learn from others.

One way to build meaningful connections through inquiry is by asking open-ended questions that encourage others to share their thoughts and experiences. For instance instead of assuming someone's motivations or beliefs you can inquire by asking "What led you to that decision?" or "What are your thoughts on this matter?" By genuinely seeking to understand others you can build rapport and create a shared space for open dialogue.

In addition to asking questions reflective listening plays a crucial role in building meaningful connections. Reflective listening involves paraphrasing and summarizing the speaker's statements to confirm understanding and demonstrate empathy. This technique shows that you value their perspective and are willing to engage in a meaningful conversation.

Furthermore building meaningful connections through inquiry requires active engagement and a willingness to suspend judgment. Instead of immediately dismissing someone's viewpoint take the time to understand their perspective and explore the underlying reasons for their opinions. This creates an environment of mutual respect and understanding where diverse perspectives are valued and appreciated.

To summarize empowering communication involves various skills and techniques that promote clarity understanding and meaningful connections. Asking for clarification and understanding helps ensure that both parties are on the same page and reduces misunderstandings. Active listening and engagement demonstrate respect and interest in the speaker's message. Effective questioning encourages deeper reflection and critical thinking. Finally building meaningful connections through inquiry fosters curiosity empathy and an appreciation of diverse perspectives. By integrating these techniques into our communication practices we can create an environment where everyone feels heard understood and empowered.

Chapter 7: Embracing Lifelong Learning

Embracing lifelong learning is a transformative mindset that recognizes knowledge as an unending journey rather than a destination. It involves the continuous pursuit of new skills, insights, and experiences throughout one's life. This commitment to learning not only broadens horizons but also nurtures adaptability and resilience in an ever-evolving world. It empowers individuals to remain curious, stay relevant, and embrace change with enthusiasm. In this lifelong pursuit of knowledge, individuals not only enrich their own lives but also contribute to the betterment of society, as they become beacons of inspiration and innovation, illuminating the path to a brighter future for themselves and those around them.

7.1 The Importance of Continuous Education

In today's rapidly changing world lifelong learning has become essential for personal and professional growth. Continuous education provides numerous benefits such as acquiring new skills expanding knowledge staying relevant in a dynamic job market and fostering personal development. It promotes adaptability creativity critical thinking and problem-solving abilities enabling individuals to thrive in an ever-evolving society.

One of the main reasons why continuous education is vital is because it helps individuals keep pace with technological advancements. In fields like IT healthcare or engineering where new technologies emerge frequently continuous learning ensures professionals remain up-to-date with the latest tools and techniques. For example a software developer who doesn't invest in continuous education may become obsolete in a few years due to shifts in programming languages and development methodologies.

Additionally continuous education allows individuals to stay competitive in the job market. Employers often prefer candidates who demonstrate a commitment to learning and who possess a diverse skill set. By constantly acquiring new knowledge and skills individuals can differentiate themselves from others and increase their chances of landing better job opportunities or advancing in their careers.

Moreover continuous education contributes to personal development by broadening perspectives and fostering intellectual growth. It enables individuals to explore new subjects cultures and ideas promoting a well-rounded understanding of the world. Lifelong learning also enhances communication skills critical thinking and problem-solving abilities enabling individuals to approach challenges from various angles and find innovative solutions.

7.2 Seeking Knowledge beyond the Classroom

While traditional educational institutions offer structured learning programs embracing lifelong learning goes beyond classroom settings. Seeking knowledge outside the confines of formal education allows individuals to explore a wide range of subjects and develop a holistic understanding of the world.

One way to seek knowledge beyond the classroom is through online resources and e-learning platforms. Nowadays the internet provides ample opportunities to access courses tutorials webinars and educational content in various formats. Websites like Coursera Udemy and Khan Academy offer a wide range of courses taught by experts from around the world. These platforms enable individuals to learn at their own pace and choose subjects that align with their interests or career goals.

Another avenue for seeking knowledge is through reading books journals and magazines. Books are a gateway to different worlds providing valuable insights into various subjects cultures and viewpoints. Whether it's non-fiction books that offer in-depth knowledge on specific topics or fictional works that spark imagination and foster empathy reading broadens horizons and stimulates intellectual growth.

Participating in workshops conferences and seminars is another excellent way to gain knowledge beyond the classroom. These events often feature industry experts thought leaders and practitioners who share their experiences and expertise. Attending such events allows individuals to network exchange ideas and gain valuable insights from professionals in their respective fields.

Moreover engaging in personal research and exploration is essential for seeking knowledge beyond the classroom. This could involve conducting experiments exploring new hobbies or immersing oneself in cultural experiences. Personal research encourages self-discovery and deepens understanding in specific areas of interest.

7.3 Engaging in Self-directed Learning

Self-directed learning is a proactive approach to education where individuals take ownership of their learning journey. It involves setting goals identifying resources and managing one's learning process. Engaging in self-directed learning enables individuals to tailor their educational experiences according to their unique needs interests and learning styles.

One of the key aspects of self-directed learning is setting goals. By defining clear objectives individuals establish a sense of purpose and direction in their learning journey. Goals could be related to acquiring new skills advancing in a specific field or broadening one's knowledge base. Setting realistic and achievable goals helps individuals stay motivated and focused on their learning endeavors.

Identifying resources is another crucial element of self-directed learning. With the abundance of information available it is essential to select reliable resources that align with your goals. These resources could include books online courses podcasts research articles or mentorship opportunities. The internet offers a multitude of platforms where individuals can access educational materials and connect with experts in their fields of interest.

Managing one's learning process is another crucial aspect of self-directed learning. Effective time management organization skills and discipline are essential to maintain a consistent and structured learning routine. Creating a schedule allotting dedicated time for learning and tracking progress are strategies that support the management of one's learning journey.

Self-reflection is also fundamental in self-directed learning. Regularly assessing one's progress identifying strengths and areas for improvement and adjusting learning strategies accordingly is key to achieving optimal results. Self-reflection encourages self-awareness and the ability to adapt and refine learning approaches as needed.

7.4 Embracing Opportunities for Growth and Development

Embracing lifelong learning involves actively seeking opportunities for growth and development. These opportunities can come in various forms and can arise from within one's current job or external sources.

One avenue for growth is through professional development programs offered by employers. Many organizations recognize the importance of investing in their employees' growth and provide training and development opportunities. These programs can include workshops seminars mentoring initiatives or tuition reimbursement for further education. By taking advantage of these opportunities individuals can enhance their skills expand their knowledge and progress within their careers.

Engaging in volunteer work or community service is another way to embrace opportunities for growth and development. Volunteering allows individuals to contribute to society while gaining new experiences and skills. It can also provide exposure to diverse perspectives and foster personal growth. Volunteering in areas that align with one's interests or align with career goals can be particularly enriching.

Networking is crucial in uncovering new opportunities for growth and development. Building relationships with professionals in one's field can provide access to knowledge mentorship and potential career advancements. Attending industry events joining professional organizations or participating in online communities are effective ways to expand professional networks.

Additionally embracing a growth mindset is essential for continuous learning and development. A growth mindset is the belief that abilities talents and intelligence can be developed through dedication effort and learning. Embracing a growth mindset enables individuals to embrace challenges persist in the face of setbacks and view failure as an opportunity for growth rather than a hindrance. This mindset fosters a lifelong commitment to learning and opens doors to new possibilities.

In conclusion embracing lifelong learning is crucial in today's ever-changing world. Continuous education provides numerous benefits such as staying relevant in the job market acquiring new skills and fostering personal development. Seeking knowledge beyond traditional classroom settings is essential as it allows for exploration of diverse subjects and perspectives. Engaging in self-directed learning empowers individuals to take ownership of their educational journey and tailor their learning experiences. Finally embracing opportunities for growth and development further enhances lifelong learning by actively seeking out new experiences investing in professional development and fostering a growth mindset. By embracing lifelong learning individuals can adapt grow and thrive in an ever-evolving world.

Chapter 8: Overcoming Obstacles to Curiosity

Overcoming obstacles to curiosity is a vital journey that enables individuals to unleash their innate thirst for knowledge and exploration. It involves identifying and surmounting the barriers that hinder curiosity, such as fear, doubt, or complacency. This endeavor requires resilience and determination, as it often involves pushing through setbacks and societal norms that discourage curiosity. By dismantling these barriers, individuals can unlock their full potential, fostering a mindset of continuous learning and discovery. In doing so, they not only enrich their own lives but also inspire others to embrace the power of curiosity, propelling collective growth and innovation.

8.1 The Fear of Failure and Judgment:

One of the biggest obstacles to curiosity is the fear of failure and judgment. Many people hesitate to explore new ideas or try new things because they are afraid of making mistakes or being seen as incompetent. This fear of failure can hold us back from being curious and exploring our interests and passions.

To overcome the fear of failure it is important to reframe failure as a learning opportunity rather than a sign of incompetence. Embracing a growth mindset which is the belief that intelligence and abilities can be developed with practice and effort can help us approach new challenges with a sense of curiosity and resilience.

Additionally seeking out supportive environments and communities can create a safe space to explore and learn without the fear of judgment. Surrounding yourself with like-minded individuals who understand the value of curiosity can foster a positive mindset and encourage exploration.

For example imagine someone who has always been interested in painting but has never pursued it due to the fear of not being good enough. By reframing failure as an opportunity for growth and joining a supportive art community or taking painting classes they can overcome their fear explore their curiosity and develop their skills and passion for painting.

8.2 Breaking Free from Comfort Zones:

Another obstacle to curiosity is the tendency to stick to our comfort zones. We often prefer to stay within familiar boundaries because they offer security and predictability. However staying within our comfort zones limits our opportunities for learning and growth.

To overcome this obstacle it is essential to intentionally step outside of our comfort zones and embrace new experiences. This can be done by seeking out new challenges trying new activities or deliberately exposing ourselves to different perspectives and ideas.

For example someone who is used to socializing within their close-knit group of friends may decide to join a club or attend social events where they can meet new people and expand their social circle. By doing so they can broaden their horizons learn from different perspectives and satisfy their curiosity about new social dynamics.

8.3 Dealing with Information Overload:

In today's age of information we are bombarded with an overwhelming amount of data and content. This information overload can make it difficult to focus on one topic or explore new ideas deeply which can hinder curiosity.

To overcome information overload it is important to cultivate the skill of selective attention and focus on the information that is most relevant and valuable to our interests and goals. Setting specific goals and limits for our information consumption can help us filter through the noise and prioritize what truly matters.

Another useful strategy is to develop critical thinking skills to evaluate the credibility and accuracy of the information we encounter. This allows us to separate reliable sources from misinformation and make well-informed decisions.

For example imagine someone interested in learning about climate change but feeling overwhelmed by the vast amount of information available. By setting specific learning objectives such as understanding the causes and effects of climate change they can filter their information searches to focus on reputable scientific sources or attend webinars hosted by experts in the field. This approach allows them to deepen their understanding and satisfy their curiosity without getting overwhelmed by excessive information.

8.4 Cultivating Resilience and Perseverance:

Curiosity often requires resilience and perseverance as it involves facing challenges setbacks and obstacles along the way. When we encounter difficulties or roadblocks our curiosity may waver and we may feel tempted to give up. However cultivating resilience and perseverance is essential to overcoming these obstacles and fostering curiosity.

To cultivate resilience and perseverance it is important to develop a growth mindset and embrace failures and setbacks as part of the learning process. Instead of viewing challenges as roadblocks we can see them as opportunities to grow and evolve. Embracing a positive attitude and maintaining a sense of optimism can help us bounce back from setbacks and keep our curiosity alive.

For example imagine someone experimenting with a new programming language who encounters multiple errors and bugs in their code. Instead of becoming discouraged they approach each error as a puzzle to solve and an opportunity to expand their knowledge. Their curiosity and determination to find the solution keeps them motivated and resilient in the face of challenges.

Additionally setting small achievable goals and celebrating milestones along the way can help maintain motivation and momentum. Breaking down larger projects or tasks into smaller manageable steps reduces feelings of overwhelm and allows us to make progress incrementally.

In conclusion overcoming obstacles to curiosity such as the fear of failure and judgment breaking free from comfort zones dealing with information overload and cultivating resilience and perseverance is crucial for personal and intellectual growth. By reframing failure stepping outside our comfort zones managing information overload and developing resilience and perseverance we can foster a lifelong love for learning exploration and curiosity.

Chapter 9: Harnessing Curiosity in the Digital Age

Harnessing curiosity in the digital age is a dynamic endeavor that involves utilizing the vast resources and opportunities available in the digital realm to fuel one's innate desire for exploration and knowledge. It requires individuals to navigate the vast sea of information with discernment, leveraging technology to seek answers, connect with diverse perspectives, and delve into new realms of understanding. In this age of instant access to information, it's crucial to balance the allure of quick answers with the deeper satisfaction that comes from in-depth exploration. By harnessing curiosity effectively in the digital age, individuals can not only satisfy their thirst for knowledge but also harness the transformative potential of technology to drive innovation, personal growth, and meaningful connections.

9.1 Navigating the Digital Landscape:

In the digital age we are constantly bombarded with an overwhelming amount of information. The internet has opened up a vast world of knowledge and resources but it can also be a breeding ground for misinformation and distractions. Navigating the digital landscape requires a critical eye and the ability to discern reliable sources from unreliable ones.

One key skill in navigating the digital landscape is information literacy. Information literacy involves the ability to locate evaluate and effectively use information from digital sources. It requires the development of skills such as searching for reliable sources identifying bias and misinformation and understanding how to ethically use and attribute information.

For example when conducting research online it is essential to evaluate the credibility of the sources you come across. Consider the author's credentials the publication or website's reputation and whether the information is supported by evidence from other reliable sources. Evaluating the accuracy and reliability of sources will help you make informed decisions and avoid falling into the trap of spreading false information.

9.2 Evaluating Online Information:

One of the challenges in the digital age is the proliferation of fake news rumors and misinformation. This makes it crucial for individuals to develop strong critical thinking skills to evaluate the information they come across online.

One important aspect of evaluating online information is considering the source. Is it from a reputable news organization or a personal blog? Is the author an expert in the field? Does the website have a clear bias? These questions can help you determine the credibility of the information you are consuming.

Additionally fact-checking is an essential skill in today's digital landscape. Fact-checking involves verifying the accuracy of claims or statements using reliable sources. There are fact-checking websites and tools available that can help you determine the truthfulness of information.

For instance when encountering a provocative claim or a sensationalized headline it is essential to fact-check the information before accepting it as true. By verifying the accuracy of the claims you can avoid spreading misinformation and enhance your understanding of the world around you.

9.3 Using Technology to Fuel Curiosity:

While the internet and technology can be distracting they also present numerous opportunities to fuel curiosity and learn. In the digital age it is important to leverage technology to enhance your understanding of a wide range of topics.

One way to use technology for curiosity is through online courses and educational platforms. Websites like Coursera edX and Khan Academy offer a wealth of courses on various subjects allowing you to delve deeper into your areas of interest. These platforms provide accessible and affordable education for people of all ages and backgrounds.

Moreover technology has made it easier than ever to connect with experts and like-minded individuals around the world. Online communities forums and social media platforms provide opportunities to engage in discussions ask questions and share knowledge. By participating in online communities you can tap into the collective wisdom and diverse perspectives of people who share your interests.

For example if you're interested in astronomy you can join online forums where amateur astronomers share their experiences knowledge and recommendations for observing celestial bodies. These interactions not only fuel curiosity but also provide a supportive network of individuals with whom you can learn and grow.

Additionally technology has made it possible to access a vast array of multimedia resources. Podcasts documentaries webinars and YouTube channels offer engaging and interactive content that can broaden your horizons and deepen your understanding of various subjects. By exploring different formats you can find the medium that best suits your learning style and preferences.

9.4 Maintaining a Healthy Balance:

While technology can be a valuable tool in fostering curiosity it is essential to maintain a healthy balance in its use. The constant access to information and the addictive nature of digital devices can lead to information overload and a loss of focus.

One way to maintain a healthy balance is by setting boundaries for technology use. Establish designated times or spaces where you disconnect from digital devices and engage in offline activities. This can help you refocus your attention engage in mindfulness and cultivate curiosity in the world around you.

Another important aspect of maintaining a healthy balance is being mindful of the content you consume. It is easy to fall into the trap of mindlessly scrolling through social media feeds or getting lost in endless YouTube videos. Instead be intentional about the content you engage with and seek out valuable and thought-provoking resources.

For instance instead of spending hours on social media allocate a portion of your time to reading books or engaging in hobbies that spark your curiosity. By diversifying your sources of information and activities you can foster a deeper understanding and enrich your overall learning experience.

Moreover it is crucial to take breaks from technology to recharge and allow your mind to wander. Engaging in activities such as going for a walk spending time in nature or practicing mindfulness can help stimulate creativity and curiosity. These breaks provide an opportunity for reflection introspection and the generation of new ideas.

In conclusion navigating the digital landscape in the digital age requires critical thinking skills and information literacy to differentiate between reliable sources and misinformation. Evaluating online information involves considering the credibility of sources and fact-checking claims to ensure accurate knowledge acquisition. Technology can be harnessed to fuel curiosity through online courses communities and multimedia resources. However maintaining a healthy balance is essential to prevent information overload and foster a meaningful engagement with the world. By setting boundaries being mindful of content and taking breaks from technology individuals can cultivate curiosity and enhance their learning experiences in the digital age.

Chapter 10: Encouraging Curiosity in Others

Encouraging curiosity in others is a powerful catalyst for fostering lifelong learning and personal growth. It involves creating an environment that values questions, exploration, and open-mindedness. By actively listening, supporting diverse interests, and providing access to resources, individuals can inspire curiosity in those around them. This encouragement not only nurtures a culture of learning but also empowers others to unlock their potential and pursue their passions. In doing so, we become advocates for curiosity, igniting a spark in others that fuels their quest for knowledge, innovation, and a deeper understanding of the world.

10.1 Fostering a Curiosity-friendly Environment:

In order to encourage curiosity in others it is important to create a curiosity-friendly environment. This involves providing individuals with the space support and resources necessary to explore their interests and ask questions. Here are a few strategies to foster a curiosity-friendly environment:

1. Encourage questioning: Encourage individuals to ask ques-

tions and challenge assumptions. Create an atmosphere where no question is considered too silly or insignificant. This helps individuals feel comfortable expressing their curiosity.

Example: In a classroom setting a teacher can dedicate a portion of the lesson to a "question and answer" session where students can ask anything related to the topic being discussed.

2. Provide resources: Make sure individuals have access to a variety of resources such as books articles videos and experts in different fields. This allows them to explore their interests and delve deeper into subjects they are curious about.

Example: A company can create a curated library with books and resources on various topics and make them easily accessible to employees.

3. Promote experimentation: Encourage individuals to experiment and try new things. Provide opportunities for hands-on experiences and support them in their efforts.

Example: An organization can organize regular "innovation sprints" where employees are given the time and resources to work on their own projects and come up with creative solutions.

4. Celebrate curiosity: Recognize and celebrate curiosity in others. Acknowledge and appreciate individuals who demonstrate a genuine curiosity for learning and encourage others to follow suit.

Example: A school can have a "curiosity wall" where students' questions and discoveries are showcased and celebrated.

10.2 Teaching Curiosity in Education:

In the realm of education teaching curiosity can have a profound impact on students' learning and academic success. By cultivating curiosity educators can enhance engagement critical thinking and problem-solving skills. Here are some ways to teach curiosity in education:

1. Inquiry-based learning: Design lessons and activities that promote inquiry and encourage students to ask questions investigate and seek answers themselves.

Example: A science teacher can assign a project where students have to choose a question they are curious about and conduct experiments to find the answers.

2. Open-ended assignments: Assign open-ended tasks that allow students to explore different perspectives and come up with unique solutions.

Example: A literature teacher can ask students to write an alternative ending to a story encouraging them to think creatively and explore beyond the existing narrative.

3. Role-model curiosity: Teachers can model curiosity by demonstrating enthusiasm for learning asking questions themselves and actively seeking knowledge.

Example: A history teacher can share their own curiosity about a particular historical event or figure showing students that even experts are continuously learning.

4. Encourage divergent thinking: Foster an environment where students feel comfortable expressing different viewpoints and thinking outside the box.

Example: A math teacher can organize a class debate where students explore different approaches to solving a problem encouraging them to think critically and consider alternative solutions.

10.3 Leadership and Curiosity:

Leaders have a significant role to play in fostering curiosity within their teams and organizations. By promoting and modeling curiosity leaders can enhance creativity innovation and problem-solving abilities. Here are some ways leaders can encourage curiosity:

1. Create a safe space: Foster a psychologically safe environment where employees feel comfortable expressing their curiosity asking questions and sharing ideas without fear of judgment or repercussions.

Example: A leader can hold regular town hall meetings where employees are encouraged to ask any question they have fostering open communication.

2. Provide learning opportunities: Offer opportunities for continuous learning and professional development. Support

employees in acquiring new skills and knowledge that align with their interests and goals.

Example: A leader can allocate a budget for employees to attend conferences workshops or online courses of their choice.

3. Reward curiosity: Recognize and reward individuals who demonstrate curiosity and actively seek knowledge or propose innovative ideas.

Example: A company can have a "curiosity award" to acknowledge employees who have made significant contributions through their curiosity and creativity.

4. Lead by example: Model curiosity as a leader by asking questions seeking feedback and demonstrating a genuine interest in learning and growth.

Example: A manager can initiate regular "learning lunches" where team members discuss and share interesting articles books or podcasts they have come across.

10.4 Inspiring a Curious Community:

Curiosity can extend beyond individual and organizational boundaries to create thriving communities that foster learning collaboration and innovation. Here are some ways to inspire a curious community:

1. Networking events: Organize networking events or gatherings where people from different backgrounds and disciplines can

come together to exchange ideas and share knowledge.

Example: A community organization can organize a monthly meet-up where experts from various fields give short talks on their areas of expertise followed by a Q&A session.

2. Collaborative projects: Encourage collaboration and interdisciplinary projects that bring together individuals from different fields to work on common goals.

Example: A community center can initiate a project that involves artists scientists and engineers working together to create an interactive exhibit for the community.

3. Sharing platforms: Create platforms where community members can share their knowledge skills and experiences with others.

Example: A neighborhood association can launch a community blog or online forum where residents can share interesting stories information and resources.

4. Public lectures/workshops: Organize public lectures or workshops led by experts in various fields to inspire curiosity and promote lifelong learning.

Example: A local library can host monthly talks where authors researchers or entrepreneurs speak about their work and engage with the community through Q&A sessions.

In conclusion fostering curiosity in others involves creating a curiosity-friendly environment teaching curiosity in education encouraging curiosity through leadership and inspiring a curious community. These strategies can have a transformative impact on individuals organizations and communities unleashing creativity innovation and growth.

Chapter 11: The Future of Curiosity

The future of curiosity holds immense promise as we continue to advance in our understanding of the human mind and the world around us. With the rapid evolution of technology, including artificial intelligence and virtual reality, opportunities for exploration and discovery will expand exponentially. However, it also brings challenges, such as information overload and potential distractions. Nurturing curiosity will require a balance between harnessing the benefits of technology while preserving the human instinct to wonder and question. The future will see curiosity as a driving force for innovation, problem-solving, and personal development, with individuals and society as a whole benefiting from its unceasing quest for knowledge and understanding.

11.1 How Curiosity Shapes Innovation:

Curiosity is a fundamental driver of innovation. It is the motivation to explore question and seek new knowledge and understanding. Without curiosity progress would be hindered and existing knowledge and technologies would stagnate.

Innovation is about finding new ways to address challenges and create solutions. It requires the ability to think creatively and critically which are fueled by curiosity. Curiosity encourages individuals to question existing assumptions explore unconventional ideas and take risks. It pushes them outside their comfort zones and opens up new possibilities for discovery.

One example of curiosity shaping innovation is the invention of the telephone. Alexander Graham Bell''s curiosity about how sound travels led him to invent the telephone which revolutionized communication. Similarly the curiosity of inventors like Thomas Edison and Nikola Tesla led to groundbreaking inventions that transformed the world.

Innovation also occurs through interdisciplinary approaches where curiosity drives individuals to explore connections between seemingly unrelated fields. For example the field of bioinformatics emerged from the curiosity of researchers who wanted to understand and analyze biological data using computational methods. This interdisciplinary approach has revolutionized biological research and led to significant breakthroughs.

Furthermore curiosity is essential in the development of new technologies. Take the example of self-driving cars. The curiosity of engineers and researchers about how to improve transportation and reduce accidents has led to the development of autonomous vehicles. Without curiosity we would not have witnessed such advancements in the automotive industry.

11.2 Curiosity and Problem-solving in a Changing World:

In a rapidly changing world curiosity plays a vital role in

problem-solving. Many of the challenges we face require innovative solutions and curiosity enables us to think beyond traditional approaches.

Curiosity helps us question the status quo and challenge existing systems and practices. It allows us to identify limitations and inefficiencies and seek alternative solutions. For example the curiosity of environmentalists about the impact of plastic waste on ecosystems led to the development of biodegradable materials as a solution.

Moreover curiosity drives us to explore emerging technologies and scientific advancements. It helps us anticipate future challenges and adapt to new circumstances. For instance the curiosity of researchers in the field of artificial intelligence has led to the development of machine learning algorithms that can analyze vast amounts of data and make predictions. These algorithms have the potential to solve complex problems in various domains such as healthcare and finance.

In a changing world curiosity also helps foster resilience and adaptability. It allows individuals to seek new knowledge and acquire the skills needed to navigate unfamiliar territories. For example the curiosity of individuals to understand emerging technologies like blockchain and cryptocurrencies has led to the creation of new industries and job opportunities.

11.3 The Role of Curiosity in Scientific Advancements:

Scientific advancements are driven by curiosity. Curiosity is at the core of the scientific method which involves asking questions formulating hypotheses designing experiments and analyzing data.

Scientific curiosity is the driving force behind exploring the unknown pushing the boundaries of knowledge and making new discoveries. For example the curiosity of scientists about the nature of light led to groundbreaking discoveries in the field of quantum mechanics.

Curiosity also plays a crucial role in scientific collaboration and interdisciplinary research. It encourages scientists from different fields to come together and share their knowledge and perspectives. This collaboration can lead to innovative solutions and a deeper understanding of complex problems.

Furthermore curiosity enables scientists to challenge established theories and paradigms. It encourages them to seek alternative explanations and explore new hypotheses. For example the curiosity of Albert Einstein about the nature of gravity led to the development of the theory of general relativity which revolutionized our understanding of the universe.

In addition to driving scientific advancements curiosity also plays a role in science communication and public engagement. Curiosity sparks interest and excitement in the general public leading to a greater appreciation and support for scientific research. It also encourages individuals to pursue scientific careers and contribute to the advancement of knowledge.

11.4 Cultivating Curiosity for a Bright Future:

Cultivating curiosity in individuals is crucial for a bright future. Curiosity fosters lifelong learning critical thinking and adaptability which are essential skills in a rapidly changing world.

One way to cultivate curiosity is through education. Curiosity can be nurtured by providing opportunities for inquiry-based learning where students are encouraged to explore their interests ask questions and seek answers. Teachers can create an environment that fosters curiosity by promoting a growth mindset encouraging students to take risks and valuing curiosity-driven exploration.

Another way to cultivate curiosity is through exposure to diverse experiences and perspectives. Traveling reading attending lectures and workshops and engaging in discussions with people from different backgrounds can fuel curiosity and expand one''s knowledge and understanding of the world.

Furthermore incorporating curiosity into the workplace can lead to innovation and creativity. Organizations can create a culture that values curiosity by encouraging employees to question existing practices explore new ideas and take calculated risks. Providing opportunities for professional development and interdisciplinary collaboration can also nurture curiosity in the workplace.

Technology can also play a role in cultivating curiosity. Online platforms and resources provide access to a vast amount of information and opportunities for exploration. Virtual reality and augmented reality technologies can create immersive learning experiences that spark curiosity and engagement.

In conclusion curiosity is a powerful force that shapes innovation problem-solving scientific advancements and the future. It is the driving force behind exploration discovery and the pursuit of knowledge. Cultivating curiosity in individuals is essential for a bright future and it can be achieved through education exposure to diverse experiences fostering a culture of curiosity in the workplace and leveraging technology. Embracing and nurturing curiosity will lead to a world where new possibilities are explored challenges are solved and progress is made.

9 788119 786190

Printed at Repro India Ltd.